The Usborne BIG book of Christmas things to make and do

Fiona Watt & Rebecca Gilpin

Designed and illustrated by
Katrina Fearn, Josephine Thompson, Antonia Miller,
Non Figg, Stella Baggot, Molly Sage, Amanda Barlow,
Kim Lane and Sue Stitt

Recipes by Catherine Atkinson
Photographs by Howard Allman
Cover design by Erica Harrison

Contents

29 Christmas decorations

Stickers

73 Christmas cards and wrapping paper

99 Christmas cooking

Fairy castle Advent calendar

1. To make the snowy hill, rip some white paper to make a curve. Glue the hill onto the bottom of a large piece of blue paper.

Make the rectangles different sizes.

2. For the towers, cut four rectangles from pink paper. Then, cut a large rectangle and two more towers from blue and purple paper.

Don't glue the large rectangle down.

3. Lay the large rectangle on the hill, to show you how wide the castle will be. Then, glue the three tallest towers onto the hill.

Large rectangle

4. Glue the large rectangle over the bottoms of the three tall towers. Then, glue the three remaining towers on top of the rectangle.

5. Cut out six different-sized triangles for the roofs of the towers. Then, glue one roof onto the top of each tower.

Don't make the shapes too small.

6. Cut out twenty-four doors for the calendar. Cut out some to go in the sky, flags for the roofs and windows for the castle.

Draw a flagpole with a silver pen.

7. Spread glue along one side of each door and glue it on. Then, under each one, draw a tiny picture or glue on a shiny sticker.

8. For the trees on the hill, cut out lots of green paper triangles. Then, glue them on, with some of them overlapping.

Print dots on some of the blue doors, too.

9. For snow, fingerprint white dots in the sky around the castle. When the paint is dry, write the numbers on the doors.

Printed penguins

1. Make a pile of several kitchen paper towels on a thick layer of old newspapers.

2. Pour some black poster paint or acrylic on top. Spread the paint with the back of a spoon.

3. Cut a big potato in half. Then, carefully cut away two sides, like this, to make a handle.

4. To print a body, press the potato into the paint then press it onto a piece of thick paper.

5. When the paint has dried, use a smaller potato to print a white tummy on the penguin.

6. Dip a brush in a little orange paint and paint a pointed beak on one side of the penguin.

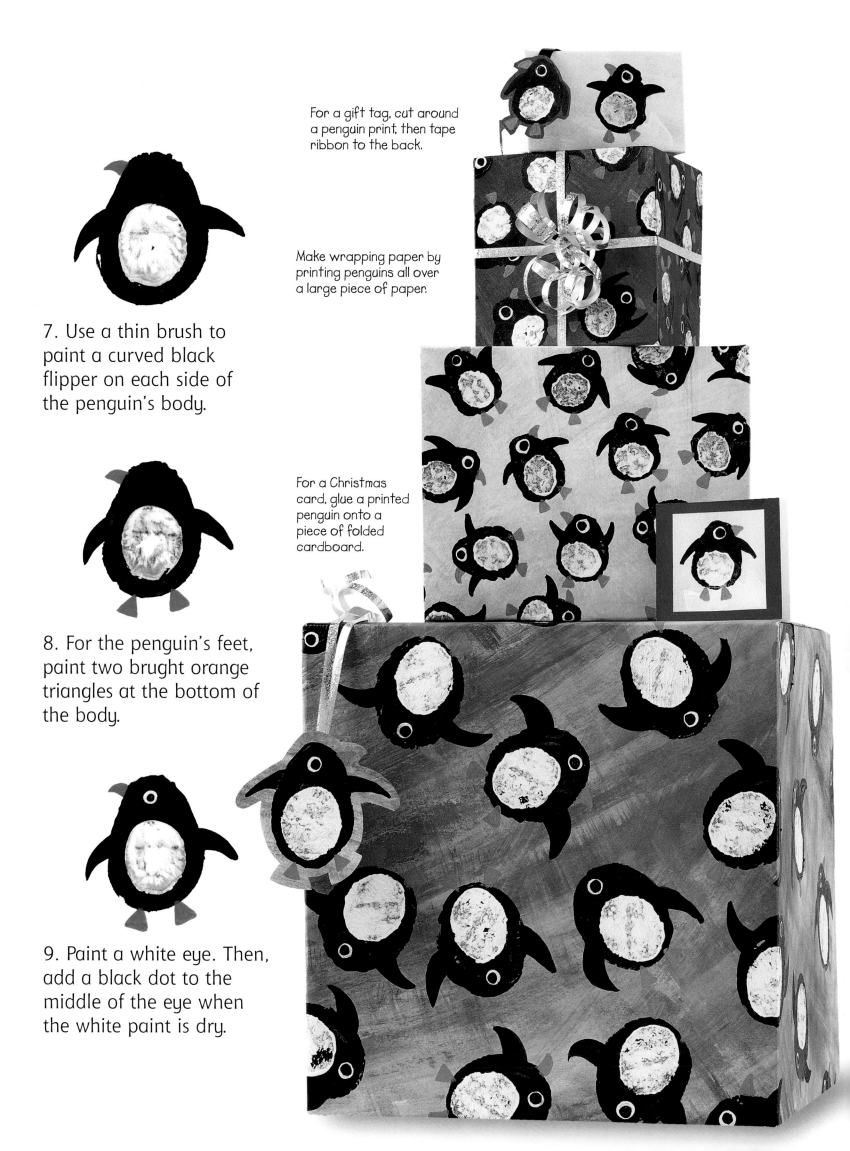

7. Use a thin brush to paint a curved black flipper on each side of the penguin's body.

8. For the penguin's feet, paint two brught orange triangles at the bottom of the body.

9. Paint a white eye. Then, add a black dot to the middle of the eye when the white paint is dry.

For a gift tag, cut around a penguin print, then tape ribbon to the back.

Make wrapping paper by printing penguins all over a large piece of paper.

For a Christmas card, glue a printed penguin onto a piece of folded cardboard.

Ice fairies

1. Pour some white paint onto an old plate. Then, cut a rectangle from thick cardboard and dip one edge into the paint.

2. To make a skirt, place the edge of the cardboard on some paper. Scrape it around, keeping the top end in the same place.

3. To make the body, dip the edge of a shorter piece of cardboard into the paint. Then, place it above the skirt and drag it across.

4. Mix some paint for the skin. Then, dip the end of another piece of cardboard into the paint. Press it onto the paper, to print arms.

5. Cut a small cardboard rectangle and print a neck and two feet. Then, dip your fingertip into the paint and print a head.

6. When the head is dry, spread a little blue paint onto the plate. Then, dip your finger into the paint and fingerprint some hair.

You could decorate the fairies' skirts with a line of glitter glue.

The part you're holding will stay sticky.

7. For the wings, sprinkle a little glitter onto some newspaper. Hold a piece of sticky tape at one end and dip it into the glitter.

8. Dip a second piece of tape into the glitter. Then, cut a corner off each piece of tape, away from the sticky end, like this.

9. Press the sticky end of the wings onto the fairy. Then, fold them back and press them down, so that the glitter is on the front.

Christmas fairy wings

1. Draw two big wing shapes and two smaller ones on paper. Then, cut them out and lay plastic food wrap over them.

2. Rip up white tissue paper and lay the pieces overlapping on the food wrap. Cover the shapes, including their edges.

3. Mix some household glue (PVA) with water so that it is runny. Then, brush the glue over the pieces of tissue paper.

4. Rip pieces of pink tissue paper, lay them on top, then brush them with glue. Add two more layers of white tissue paper and glue.

Put the wings on your back and ask someone to tie the ribbons around your arms at the front.

5. Sprinkle glitter over the wet glue on the wings. Let it dry, then brush another layer of glue over the top of the glitter. Leave it to dry.

6. Peel the wings off the food wrap. Lay the paper wing shapes on top, then draw around them. Cut out the shapes you have drawn.

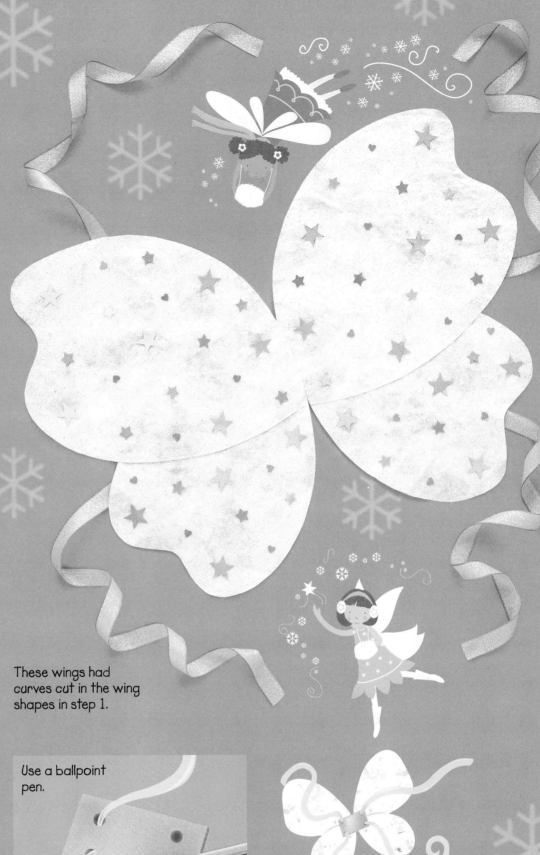

These wings had curves cut in the wing shapes in step 1.

7. Glue the top parts of the wings onto the bottom parts. Decorate the wings with sequins, stickers or shiny paper shapes.

Use a ballpoint pen.

8. Cut a small rectangle from thick cardboard. Make four holes in it with a pen, then thread two long pieces of ribbon through the holes.

Leave long ends on the ribbons.

9. Glue the rectangle onto the back of the wings, with the ends of the ribbons sticking out. Then, let the glue dry completely.

11

Fairy crown

Draw the line a little way from the bottom.

1. Cut a rectangle of paper that fits around your head. This crown sits on the top of your head, so cut a little off one end.

2. Fold the rectangle in half, with the short ends together, then fold it twice more. Then, draw a line across the paper, like this.

Use hair clips to clip the crown to your hair.

Crease mark

Cut through all the layers.

3. To mark the middle of the folded paper, fold it in half, with the long sides together. Then, press it to make a crease at the end.

4. Using a ruler, draw a line from the crease mark to each end of the line at the bottom. Then, cut along the slanting lines.

5. Unfold the paper shape, then lay it on a piece of thin cardboard. Carefully draw around the shape, and cut it out.

The cut goes halfway down.

6. Cut off the triangle at one end, leaving a strip at the bottom. Then, make a cut down into the strip, like this.

7. At the other end of the crown, make a cut up into the last triangle, like this. Make the cut the same length as the first one.

8. Bend the crown around and slot the cuts into each other, with the ends inside. Then, secure the ends with a piece of tape.

Glue little beads onto
the ends of the points.

9. Bend each point out
with your fingers, like this.
Then, glue beads and
sequins onto the crown, or
decorate it with glitter glue.

13

Handprinted angel

This is the angel's dress upside-down.

1. For the dress, press your hand in blue paint, then press it in the middle of some paper.

2. Press both hands into some yellow paint. Make two prints a little lower, for the wings.

3. Turn your paper. Dip your finger in pink paint, then go around and around, for a head.

4. Use your fingertip to do blue arms. Join them to the dress. Add some hands, too.

5. Use orange paint to finger paint some hair. Then, add a yellow halo above the head.

6. Fingerprint some eyes and a nose. Then, use your little fingertip to paint a smiling mouth.

Glue your angel
picture to a piece of
stiff paper to make a
large Christmas card.

15

Christmas tree advent calendar

1. Cut a piece of bright cardboard or thick paper the same size as this book, when it's opened out.

2. For the tree, fold a large rectangle of green paper in half, long sides together.

3. Draw a diagonal line, then cut along it. Cut out small triangles along the open edge.

You will need 24 altogether.

Glue down here only.

4. Cut a white shape for the snow. Glue it on. Open out the tree and glue it in the middle.

5. For the 'doors', draw different shapes. You could also use stickers from the sticker pages.

6. Cut out all the shapes you have drawn. Put glue along one edge of each shape and press it on.

Make sure your picture is smaller than the door.

7. Draw a small Christmas picture behind each door, or press on a sticker from the sticker pages.

8. Decorate the tree around the doors with extra stickers and shapes cut from paper.

9. Use a felt-tip pen to write a number on each door. Start at one and go up to 24.

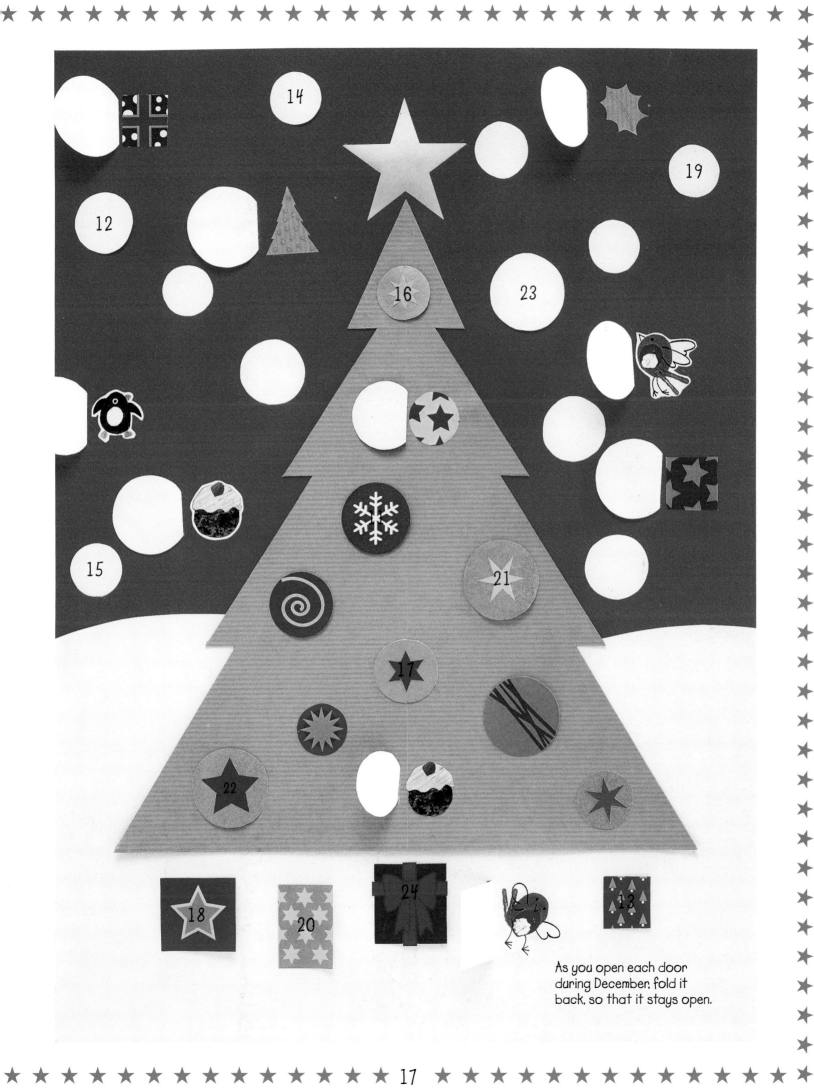

As you open each door during December, fold it back, so that it stays open.

Spangly star wand

1. Draw a star on a piece of cardboard and cut it out. Then, put the star onto the cardboard again and draw around it.

This wand was made using bits of blue and white tissue paper.

These wands had shiny paper glued around the straw, instead of foil.

Keep the marks at the top of the stars.

2. Draw a mark at the top of the first star, then move it off the cardboard. Draw a mark at the top of the second star, then cut it out.

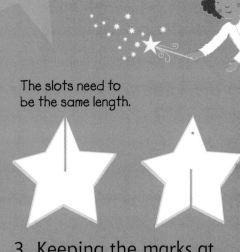

The slots need to be the same length.

3. Keeping the marks at the top, cut a slot in each star, like this. Make the slots the same thickness as the cardboard.

4. Cut a rectangle from a roll of kitchen foil, making it a little longer and several times wider than a drinking straw.

5. Lay the foil on some old newspaper and cover the non-shiny side with glue. Then, lay the straw on top, near one edge of the foil.

Squash the end of the straw.

6. Roll the straw, so that the foil sticks all the way around it. Then, tape the straw onto the star with a slot at the top.

Hold the straw in place.

7. Hold the star with the slot at the bottom, above the star with the slot at the top. Then, push the stars together, like this.

Use household glue (PVA).

8. Rip up lots of strips of tissue paper and glue them all over the stars. Cover the stars with two or three layers of tissue paper.

9. Brush the stars with glue and sprinkle them with glitter. Glue on lots of beads and sequins, or shapes cut from shiny paper.

Holly fairy collage

Join the points in the middle.

1. For the fairy's skirt, rip a shape from pink paper. Don't worry if it's uneven. Glue it onto a piece of paper for the background.

2. For the wings, cut green pictures out of a magazine. Fold them in half and draw half a holly leaf on the fold. Then, cut out the leaves.

3. Unfold the leaves and flatten them. Then, glue them onto the background, just above the top of the fairy's skirt.

4. Rip a shape that is a little bigger than the skirt, from white tissue paper. Then, gather the tissue paper at the top, like this.

You could make a holly fairy and glue it to the front of a card.

5. Glue the gathered part of the white tissue paper onto the skirt. Then, cut out a body from white paper and glue it on top.

Use paper from a magazine.

6. Cut out a head, a neck and some hair. Glue the head and neck onto the hair, then draw a face. Glue the head onto the body.

Glue the feet onto some shoes.

7. Cut out arms and rip sleeves from paper. Glue them all onto the fairy. Then, cut out feet and glue them on, too.

Decorate the dress, too.

8. Cut a crown and a strip of paper for a wand and glue them onto the fairy. Add a star sequin or sticker to the end of the wand.

Printed reindeer

1. Cut a potato in half, lengthways. Then, turn it over and cut away two pieces at the sides, to make a handle.

2. Lay a few kitchen paper towels in a pile on a newspaper. Pour brown paint on top and spread it out with an old spoon.

3. Holding the handle, press the flat side of the potato firmly onto the patch of brown paint, then lift it up.

4. Press the potato onto some paper to print the reindeer's head. Press the potato into the paint again and do more prints.

5. For the reindeer's ears, dip your finger into the brown paint. Fingerprint an ear on either side of the head.

6. When the brown paint is dry, pour red paint onto the paper towels and spread it out. Dip your first finger into the paint.

7. Fingerprint a red nose near the bottom of each head. Then, use a black felt-tip pen to draw two eyes on each one.

8. When the paint is dry, draw two long lines for antlers. Then, draw a few smaller lines on each side of the long lines.

You could print the reindeer
on a card or gift tag, or just
do them on paper for fun.

23

Snowflake fairies

1. Lay a mug on a piece of white paper. Draw around it, then draw around it on some purple paper, too. Then, cut out the circles.

2. To make a snowflake for the dress, fold the white circle in half, then fold it in half twice more. Then, cut a triangle out of one side.

3. Cut out lots more triangles, all around the edges of the folded piece of paper. Make the triangles different sizes.

4. Brush household glue (PVA) over the snowflake. Sprinkle it with glitter, then let it dry. Then, glue it onto the purple circle.

Body

Skirt

5. Cut the snowflake in half. For a skirt, cut one half into two pieces. Then, cut a shape for the body from the smaller piece.

6. Glue the skirt onto a piece of paper, then glue on the body. Cut out a purple sash and glue it on, where the pieces join.

The fold needs to be on this side.

7. For the wings, draw around the mug and cut out the circle. Fold it in half three times, then draw half a wing shape, like this.

You could make a
Christmas card
with a snowflake
fairy on it.

Keep the
paper folded.

Add glittery
shoes,
too.

8. Cut along the line you have drawn, then cut a few triangles along the fold, like this. Then, open out the wings.

9. Spread glue over the wings. Sprinkle them with glitter, then let the glue dry. Glue the wings next to the body, like this.

10. Cut out a head and some hair and glue them together. Cut out arms, legs and a crown and glue them all on. Then, draw a face.

Glittery fairy bookmark

1. Cut a circle from paper for the fairy's head. Then, draw a shape for the hair on thick pink paper and cut it out.

Use household glue (PVA).

2. Cover the hair with glue and sprinkle it with glitter. While the glue dries, cut a strip from the pink paper and glue the head onto it.

3. Glue the hair onto the head and draw a face. Then, cut a crown from shiny paper and glue it onto the hair.

Fold —

Use shiny paper if you have some.

4. For wings, fold a piece of thick paper in half and draw a wing on it, like this. Then, keeping the paper folded, cut out the shape.

5. Glue the wings onto the back of the pink strip of paper. Then, decorate the bookmark with stickers, glitter glue and silver pens.

The snowflakes on the blue bookmark were drawn with a silver pen.

Pretty boxes

1. Rip some tissue paper into pieces. Brush the pieces with household glue (PVA) and press them all over a box and its lid.

2. Brush glue all over the top and the sides of the lid. Then, sprinkle glitter all over the lid and leave it to dry.

3. When the glue is dry, glue sequins around the edge of the lid. Then, glue sequins in the middle too. Leave the glue to dry.

You could use any small box, such as a gift box.

27

Fingerprint fat robins

Dip your finger in paint each time you do a print.

1. Dip the end of one finger in brown paint. Print it onto paper. Do several more prints.

2. Dip a finger into red paint and press it onto each brown shape for a tummy.

3. Wash your hands. Then, dip a finger in white paint and print a spot inside the red shape.

4. Dip the edge of a piece of thin cardboard into brown paint and print two lines for the tail.

5. When the paint is completely dry, draw the robin's beak and eyes with a felt-tip pen.

6. Draw two wings and legs. For the feet, add three small lines at the end of each leg.

You could print robins on a piece of folded thick paper to make a Christmas card.

Christmas decorations

Flying angels

1. Draw a curved triangle on thick paper for the angel's dress and cut it out. Cut two arms from the same paper, too.

To make an angel's star, like this, press two stickers together, one on each side of the hand.

2. Cut out hands and glue them on the arms. Glue one arm behind the dress and glue the other arm on top of the dress.

3. Cut a round head and some hair from paper. Glue the hair onto the head, then glue the head onto the dress.

To make a wing like this angel's, glue gold paper onto the rectangle before you fold it into a zigzag.

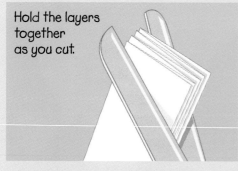

Hold the layers together as you cut.

4. Fold a rectangle of paper one way, then the other, to make a zigzag for the wing. Then, cut off the end at an angle.

5. Cut a piece of thread and tie a big knot in one end. Lay the thread in the middle of the zigzag. Then, wrap tape around the end.

6. Hold the wing against the dress, like this. Get someone to help you put a piece of tape across the wing to secure it.

30

For a sparkly halo, bend a piece of a pipe cleaner into a circle and tape it on.

7. Draw a face on your angel. Then, cut out feet and glue them on the dress. Decorate the angel with paper and stickers.

Hang your angel from a Christmas tree or as a decoration in a window.

31

Glittery star chains

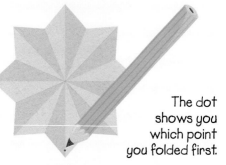

1. To make a star, put a mug on a piece of paper and draw around it with a pencil. Then, cut out the circle you have drawn.

Cut the paper at an angle, like this.

2. Fold the circle in half, then fold it in half three more times. Then, cut across the folded piece of paper, to make a point.

The dot shows you which point you folded first.

3. Unfold the star. Draw a pencil dot on one of the points. Then, fold the star in half from this point to the point opposite it.

4. Crease the fold, then open out the star. Fold the next point over to the point opposite it. Then, fold the others in the same way.

Press lightly, or you will squash the star.

5. To make a dip between two points, push the points together. Squash down the fold between them. Repeat this all the way around.

6. Unfold the star and gently press down on its middle, to open out the points a little. Then, make more stars for the chain.

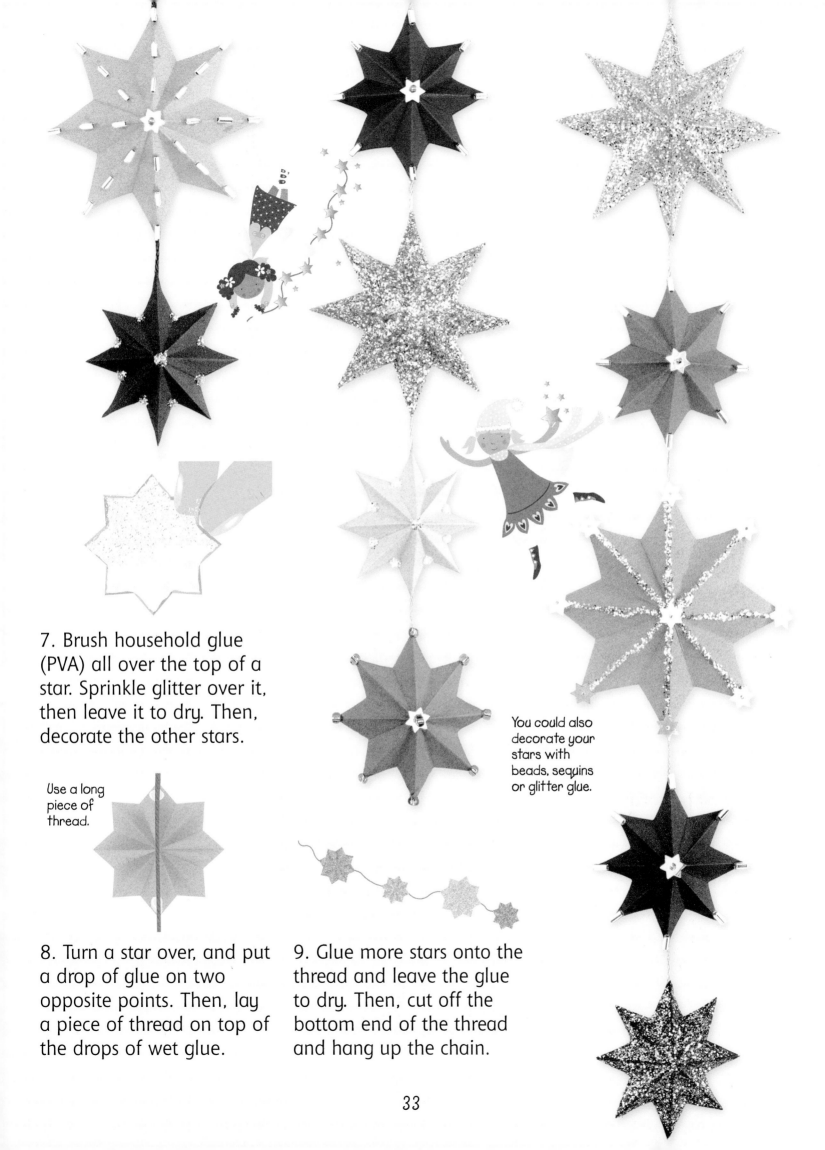

7. Brush household glue (PVA) all over the top of a star. Sprinkle glitter over it, then leave it to dry. Then, decorate the other stars.

Use a long piece of thread.

You could also decorate your stars with beads, sequins or glitter glue.

8. Turn a star over, and put a drop of glue on two opposite points. Then, lay a piece of thread on top of the drops of wet glue.

9. Glue more stars onto the thread and leave the glue to dry. Then, cut off the bottom end of the thread and hang up the chain.

Fairy lantern decorations

Mix the glue and water on an old plate.

1. Mix some household glue (PVA) with water, so that it is runny. Then, brush the glue all over one side of a piece of paper.

2. Sprinkle silver glitter over the wet glue, then leave the glue to dry. When it is dry, turn the paper over.

3. Mix some pink paint with a little water. Then, paint all over the piece of paper and leave the paint to dry completely.

Fold

You don't need these pieces.

4. When the paint is dry, draw little dots all over it with glitter glue. Then, draw a pencil line down the middle of the paper.

5. Draw three lines across the paper, to make eight rectangles the same size. Then, cut along all the lines you have drawn.

6. Fold one of the rectangles in half, along its length. With the fold at the top, cut a triangle off each end.

The cuts need to be at an angle.

Hold the ends together until they stick.

Tape this end, too.

7. Cut lots of slits along the folded edge of the paper, but don't cut as far as the unfolded side. Then, open out the paper shape.

8. Put a drop of glue at the top and bottom of one end of the shape. Bend the shape around until the ends meet. Press them together.

9. Tape a piece of thread inside the lantern, as a handle for hanging. Then, make more lanterns from the other rectangles.

Find out how to make this fairy tree decoration on pages 48-49.

The pink lantern below had a line of glitter glue added before it was glued together.

Tree and snowflake decorations

1. Fold a rectangle of green paper in half, long sides together.

Fold

2. Draw a line from the top of the fold to the opposite corner.

3. Cut along the line to make a tall triangle. Keep the paper folded.

4. Cut a triangle in the folded edge. Then, cut one in the other side.

5. Keep on cutting out triangles along one side, then the other.

6. Carefully open out the tree shape and smooth the fold flat.

Snowflake

1. Use a pencil to draw around a mug on white paper. Cut out the circle.

2. Fold the circle in half. Then, fold it in half again, like this.

3. Cut out small triangles from around the edges. Then, open it out.

36

Press small pieces of
poster tack onto the tree
and snowflakes. Press
them onto a window.

Make lots of snowflakes
and scatter them
around the trees.

Glue on sequins or
your own shiny
stickers.

Christmas collage

1. Draw a line down the middle of a large piece of thick red paper. Draw two lines across it so that you have six squares.

2. Put a piece of green paper under one corner. Line up the edges with the pencil lines and draw around the corner, like this.

3. Cut along the pencil lines to make a square. Then, draw around the square on two different shades of green paper.

4. Cut out the green squares. Glue all the squares on the red paper. Trim the edges if you need to.

5. Decorate each square with a different Christmas picture such as a star, a tree or holly. Cut them from paper or fabric.

6. To make a fan-shaped bird's tail, fold a piece of paper one way then the other to make a zigzag. Glue it at one end only.

7. Add little details to each picture with glitter, glitter glue and sequins, or glue on pieces of shiny wrapping paper.

8. Turn your collage over, then cut four strips of green paper. Fold each strip in half and tape them along the top.

9. Push a long piece of thread, ribbon or string through each paper loop. Then, tie a double knot in the thread.

Use pieces of shiny wrapping paper.

Decorate your collage with stickers from the sticker pages.

If you don't have fabric, use patterned paper from old magazines.

39

Snowman paperchain

1. Lay two pieces of thin paper with their short sides touching. Join them together with tape.

2. Fold the paper in half. Then, fold each side of the papper again so that you make a zigzag shape.

3. Use a pencil to draw a snowman's hat at the top of the paper. Draw a head below the hat.

4. Draw a band all the way across the paper. This band will be the snowman's arms.

5. Add a big, round tummy. Draw in some fat legs. Then, add two feet to the legs.

6. Draw around the shape with a felt-tip pen. Cut out the snowman out along the felt-tip pen lines.

Don't cut along the folds.

7. Open out the shape. Fill in the hats and add faces. Decorate each one in a different way.

You can join your snowmen into one long chain and hang them up.

Mini fairy garland

1. Using a pencil, draw a small heart and a slightly larger one on two shades of pink paper. Then, cut them out.

2. Glue the smaller heart onto the bigger one. Then, using glitter glue, draw around the edge of the smaller heart.

Make your garland from lots of different shapes using ideas from these pages.

3. Brush household glue (PVA) all over a small piece of bright pink paper. Sprinkle glitter over the top and let the glue dry.

4. When the glue is completely dry, turn the piece of paper over. Draw a bell on the back, then cut it out.

Decorate the glittery side.

5. Cut a paper shape that will fit across the top of the bell and glue it on. Then, decorate the bell with dots of glitter glue.

Some of these shapes were decorated with sequins and glitter glue.

The tape stops the shapes from sliding down the ribbon.

6. Draw three stars on different shades of purple paper. Cut them out, then glue them together, with the smallest one on top.

7. To hang the shapes, cut pieces of ribbon and fold them in half. Then, tape the ribbons on, to make a loop.

8. Thread the shapes onto a long piece of ribbon and space them out. Then, tape them to the long ribbon with narrow pieces of tape.

Pipe cleaner trees

The star on this tree was cut out from holographic paper.

Fold the paper in half, like this.

1. Cut a piece of wrapping paper just over the height of this page and half its width. Fold it in half, with the pattern on the inside.

2. Find the middle of the fold by bending it in half, but not actually creasing it. Then, pinch the fold to mark the middle.

Keep the paper folded as you cut.

3. Draw a line from the middle mark to each corner. Then, cut along the lines to make two triangular trees.

4. Bend the end of a pipe cleaner around to make a loop. Then, cut across the top of the trees to make two small triangles.

Shiny wrapping paper with simple patterns, like these stars, works well.

5. Spread glue on one of the triangles, then lay the pipe cleaner on top. Glue the other one and press it on, matching the edges.

You could hang these decorations on a Christmas tree or on some branches.

44

Leave a
small gap.

6. Hold the trees together and cut across again to make two strips. Glue the strips on either side of the pipe cleaner.

7. Continue cutting strips across the trees and gluing them on until they are almost at the bottom of the pipe cleaner.

8. Cut out a pot from some folded wrapping paper and glue the pieces on. Add star stickers on either side of the top of the tree.

Use stickers from the sticker pages and glitter to decorate plain paper.

Make lots of
decorations using
different shapes of
cookie cutters.

Glittering shapes

1. Press a big cookie cutter firmly into a slice of white bread.

2. Push the bread shape out of the cutter very carefully.

3. Press the end of a straw into one of the points on the star to make a hole.

4. Lift the bread shape onto a baking rack. Leave it overnight. It will get hard. Cut out more shapes.

5. Mix a little paint with household glue (PVA). Paint around the edges of the shape.

6. Paint the top of the shape. When it is dry, turn it over and paint the other side.

These bread shapes are for decoration only. Do not eat them.

Hang these on your Christmas tree or use them as hanging decorations.

7. Glue lots of glitter onto the top of the shape. Add sequins and lots of tiny beads, too.

8. Push a long piece of thread through the hole. Make a loop at the end of the thread.

9. Push the ends of the thread through the loop. Then, make a knot and pull it tight.

You could make a sparkly star for the top of your tree (see pages 60-61).

Hang the fairies on a tree with lots of other decorations.

Fairy tree decorations

1. Draw around a mug on some paper. Cut out the circle, then fold it in half. Then, unfold the circle and cut along the fold.

Use a silver pen if you have one.

2. Draw two arms on one of the half-circles and cut them out. Decorate them with a pen. Then, cut out hands and glue them on.

3. For the body, decorate the second half-circle. Then, to make it into a cone, glue halfway along its straight edge.

Hole

Make sure the decoration is on the outside.

4. Bend the paper around and press the straight edges together until they stick. Then, cut off the top of the cone, to make a tiny hole.

Cut through both layers.

Fold

5. Fold two pieces of paper in half. Draw hair on one and draw a wing on the other, touching the fold. Then, cut out the shapes.

6. Draw a face and cut it out. Glue it onto one of the hair shapes. Then, cut a long piece of thread and fold it in half.

If the knot slips through the hole, make a second knot.

7. Halfway down the piece of thread, tie a knot, to make a loop. Then, push the loop through the hole in the top of the body.

8. Glue the arms onto the body. Glue the loop onto the back part of the hair, then glue the face on top. Glue on the wings.

9. For shoes, thread small beads onto the two pieces of thread hanging down. Then, tie knots below the beads to secure them.

Sparkly garland

Decorate your ornaments with stickers from the sticker pages.

1. For a round ornament, draw around a mug on a piece of bright paper. Draw a small shape at the top for hanging.

2. Cut out the ornament. Then, cut a strip of paper and glue it across the middle. Press on stickers or glue on shiny paper.

3. For the hanger, draw a rectangle with a circle on top, on shiny paper. Cut it out, then cut a zigzag along the bottom.

You could use scraps of shiny wrapping paper to decorate some of the ornaments.

4. Fold the paper and snip a piece out of the middle of the circle to make a hole. Glue the hanger on the top of the ornament.

This tree was decorated with sequins as well as a sticker and glitter.

5. Draw a long, thin ornament. Cut three curved strips and glue them on. Make a hanger for the top and glue it on.

6. Spread stripes of glue across the ornament, then sprinkle it with glitter. Shake off any extra glitter when the glue is dry.

7. Use a hole punch to make a hole at the top of a tree, cut from green paper. Cut a rectangle of paper and glue it on the bottom.

8. Decorate the tree with paper shapes, stickers and sequins. You could also add dots of glitter or glitter glue.

The tape stops the shapes from slipping.

9. Push a piece of ribbon, thread or string through each ornament. Secure them to the ribbon with a tiny piece of tape.

Christmas beads

Use a glue stick if you have one.

1. Cut a piece of wrapping paper as long as a fat straw. Make the paper about the same height as your little finger.

2. Cover the back of the paper with glue. Then, lay the straw along one edge. Roll the paper tightly around the straw.

3. Cover more straws with different wrapping papers. For a very long chain, you will need about five straws.

You could thread ordinary beads between your paper beads.

4. When the glue is dry, cut the straws into different sizes of beads. Cut some long beads and some short ones.

5. Carefully thread a thick blunt needle with strong thread. Then, tape the long end of the thread onto a work surface.

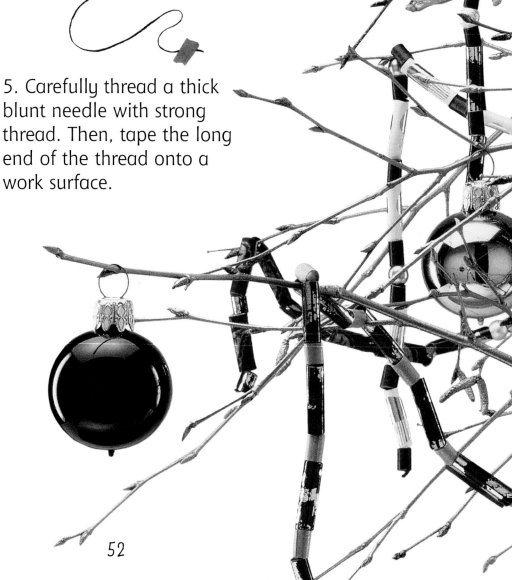

6. Thread on the beads until you have used them all. Put the needle through the last bead again and then tie a knot. Tie the thread onto the first bead in the same way.

Silver trees and birds

1. Cut a large piece of foil from a roll of kitchen foil. Spread glue all over the non-shiny side, then fold the foil in half.

2. Put the folded foil onto an old magazine. Rub the foil with your hand so that it sticks together and the surface is smooth.

Use a glue stick.

3. For a tree, draw a triangle on the foil with a ballpoint pen. Press hard as you draw. Then, draw a tree trunk at the bottom.

4. Draw a line down the middle of the tree, then add more lines for the branches. Draw lots of little lines on each branch.

5. Turn the foil over to see the raised lines. Draw more trees, then cut them out, a little way away from their outline.

6. Cut a piece of thread and fold it in half. Tape the ends to the back to make a loop for hanging your decoration.

Birds

1. Draw the outline of a bird's body and beak on the foil. Add wings, an eye and two legs. Don't forget to press hard.

2. Add some lines for the tail, making them end with a curl. Add more curved lines on the head, wings and on the tummy.

3. Cut around the bird a little way away from the lines you have drawn. Then, tape some thread on the back for hanging.

Christmas stockings

1. Fold a piece of paper as large as this page, in half, like this.

2. Use a pencil to draw a large stocking shape against the fold.

3. Cut out the stocking, but don't cut along the folded edge.

Roll little pieces of tissue paper into balls and glue them on.

Draw shapes with glue and sprinkle on lots of glitter, or use glitter glue.

Tape on a loop of thread and hang the stockings on your Christmas tree.

Don't glue along the top.

4. Open the stocking. Glue around one side, then fold the front over.

5. Rub your hand over the edge you have glued to flatten it.

6. Decorate your stocking using lots of stickers, glitter and pens.

You could put a candy cane or a small chocolate bar inside each stocking.

You could decorate a stocking with stickers from the sticker pages in this book.

Glittering snowflakes

1. Lay an old CD on a piece of thin white paper and draw around it with a pencil. Cut out the circle you have drawn.

2. Fold the paper circle in half, then fold it in half again. Then, fold the shape in half again, so that it looks like this.

CDs often come free with magazines or through the mail to advertise things. You could use one of these.

3. Use scissors to cut a 'V' shape in the tip of the folded circle. Then, cut lots of little triangles around the edges.

4. Gently unfold the paper to see your snowflake. Lay it on a flat surface and smooth it as flat as you can with your fingers.

5. Lay the CD on scrap paper and brush some runny glue around the middle of it. Sprinkle it with glitter and let it dry.

6. Shake any extra glitter off the CD. Then, put lots of little dots of glue on one side of the snowflake and press it on the CD.

7. Let the glue dry, then cut a long piece of thread and tape it to the back. You could then glue another snowflake on top.

These decorations were hung from thick shiny thread.

These decorations look best if you hang them in a place where there is lots of light.

59

Sparkly hanging hearts

1. Fold a piece of thin cardboard in half. Draw half a heart on it, like this. Keeping the cardboard folded, cut out the shape.

Fold —

2. Lay the cardboard heart on some thick paper. Draw around it four times. Then, cut out all the hearts you have drawn.

3. Fold each heart in half, from top to bottom. Then, open them out. Paint one side of one of the hearts with household glue (PVA).

4. Sprinkle glitter over the glue and leave it to dry. Then, do the same to the remaining three hearts and let the glue dry.

5. When the glue is dry, fold the hearts so that the glitter is on the inside. Then, spread glue on one half of one of the hearts.

6. Press one half of another heart onto the glue, matching the curved edge and the fold, like this. Hold it until it sticks.

7. Spread glue on the other half of the heart and press on another heart. Then, make a loop in a piece of thread and tape it inside.

8. Spread glue on both halves of the last heart and press it on, over the thread. While the glue dries, make more heart decorations.

Make lots of different-shaped decorations (see 'Other ideas' opposite).

Other ideas

Make snowflakes, circles and stars by drawing other shapes on the folded cardboard.

This shape makes a circle with a hole in the middle.

This will be a snowflake.

This shape makes a star.

Bouncing snowman

To make your snowman bounce, pull one of its boots gently, then let go.

This snowman's scarf was made from strips of paper.

Glue buttons cut from paper onto the snowman's tummy.

Make the lines about two finger widths apart

1. For the body, draw around a large plate on a piece of thin white paper. Cut out the circle you have drawn and fold it in half.

2. Draw a line from the fold of the circle almost to the edge. Then, draw one from the edge almost to the fold, like this.

3. Then, draw another line coming from the fold almost to the edge. Make this two finger widths below the second line.

4. Continue to draw lines from the fold, then from the edge. Then, cut along the pencil lines, keeping the paper folded.

5. Unfold the circle and flatten it. Then, draw around a saucer for the head. Cut it out and glue it onto the body.

6. Cut a hat from a piece of black paper and glue it on. Draw on eyes and a mouth with felt-tip pens, and glue on a paper nose.

7. Cut out arms, like sticks, from black paper and glue them on the back of the body. Cut out boots and glue them on, too.

8. Cut a piece of thread or ribbon and tape it to the back of the hat. Hold the snowman's hat and gently pull the body to stretch it.

9. Before you hang your snowman press some poster tack onto the bottom of the body. This will help it bounce.

Simple snowflakes

Use a ballpoint pen.

Curl this end around for hanging.

1. Cut a piece of cellophane from some packaging. Put a saucer on top and draw around it. Cut out the circle.

2. Cut a piece of string wider than the circle. Paint it with household glue (PVA) and press it on the cellophane, like this.

For silver string, mix the glue with silver paint.

3. Cut two more pieces of string about the width of the circle. Paint them with glue. Lay them over the first one in an 'X' shape.

Use stickers from the sticker pages to decorate the snowflakes.

4. When the glue is dry, decorate the snowflake with sequins or stickers. Tie some thread around the loop for hanging.

64

Robin decorations

1. Cut a strip of white paper about the height of this book. Bend it around to make an oval and glue it together, like this.

2. For the eye, cut a short strip of white paper. Roll it around a pencil and glue the end. Glue it inside the body.

You could hang these decorations in a window or on a Christmas tree.

3. Cut a strip of paper for the beak. Fold it in half, then bend a little bit back at each end. Glue the ends onto the body.

4. Then, cut a strip of red paper. Bend it into a teardrop shape and glue the ends. Glue it inside for the bird's tummy.

5. Glue on a strip for a tail. Make two small cuts in it, then curl the end around a pencil. Tape on some thread for hanging.

Paper angels

You could draw around a large coin.

1. Put a small plate onto a piece of thick paper. Then, use a pencil to draw around it.

2. Cut out the circle you have drawn. Then, draw a faint line across the middle of the circle.

3. For the head, draw a small circle in the middle of the big circle, just above the line, like this.

Cut along this line.

4. Draw a line around the circle. Then, draw a line from the edge to the head and cut along it.

5. Draw two curved lines, one on either side of the line across the middle. Cut out the shapes.

These will be the wings.

6. Draw four triangles around the edge, like this, then cut them out. These make the wings.

Arms   Head

Don't cut this part.

7. Cut around the arms and the head, shown here in red. Don't cut through the neck.

8. Erase any pencil lines you can see. Then, fold the wings and the arms forward. Crease them well.

9. Decorate the angel with felt-tip pens, or draw shapes with glue and sprinkle them with glitter.

Use thick white or cream paper to make the angels.

Use gold paper or foil to make the halos.

Decorate the angels' skirts with stars and spirals.

10. Turn the angel around and bend the ends around to make a cone. Tape the ends together.

11. To make a halo, fold a piece of paper in half. Draw the shape shown here and cut it out.

12. Open out the halo and flatten the fold. Tape the halo to the back of the angel's head.

Use glitter glue, if you have it, to add dots to the angels' skirts.

Snowflake baubles

1. Draw around a mug twice on a piece of white paper, then draw around it twice on red paper. Cut out the circles.

2. Cut a strip of thick cardboard about the width of one of the circles. Cut two shorter, narrower strips, too.

3. Pour some red and white paint onto an old plate. Dip the edge of the longest piece of cardboard into the white paint.

4. Press the edge onto one of the red circles. Print two more lines in an 'X', dipping the cardboard into the paint each time.

5. Use the other pieces of cardboard to print shorter lines on the snowflake. Then, print a snowflake on the other red circle.

Use other edges of the cardboard for the red paint.

6. Print red snowflakes in the same way on the white circles, then leave them until the paint is completely dry.

7. Fold each circle in half, along one of the long printed lines. Then, spread glue on one half of one of the red circles.

For a sparkly
snowflake, like
the one at the top,
print the lines with glue
and sprinkle them with glitter.

8. Press one half of a white circle onto the glue, matching the edge and the fold. Then, spread glue on its other half.

9. Press on the other red circle, matching the edge and fold as before. Then, make a loop in a piece of thread and tape it inside.

10. Glue one half of one of the red circles and press on the remaining white circle. Then, glue the last two halves together.

Tree-top fairy

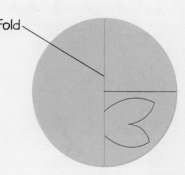

1. Lay a plate on some paper and draw around it. Cut out the circle. Then, fold the circle in half and open it out.

Find out how to make these tree decorations on pages 60-61 and page 72.

Fold

2. Using a pencil, draw a line from the middle of the circle to its edge. Then, draw a wing below the line, touching the fold.

Cut here.

3. Cut up along the fold, around the wing, along the fold again and along the line. Then, cut halfway down the wing, like this.

Line up this edge and the fold.

4. Bend the wing over and gently hold it down, like this. Then, carefully draw around the edge of the wing with a pencil.

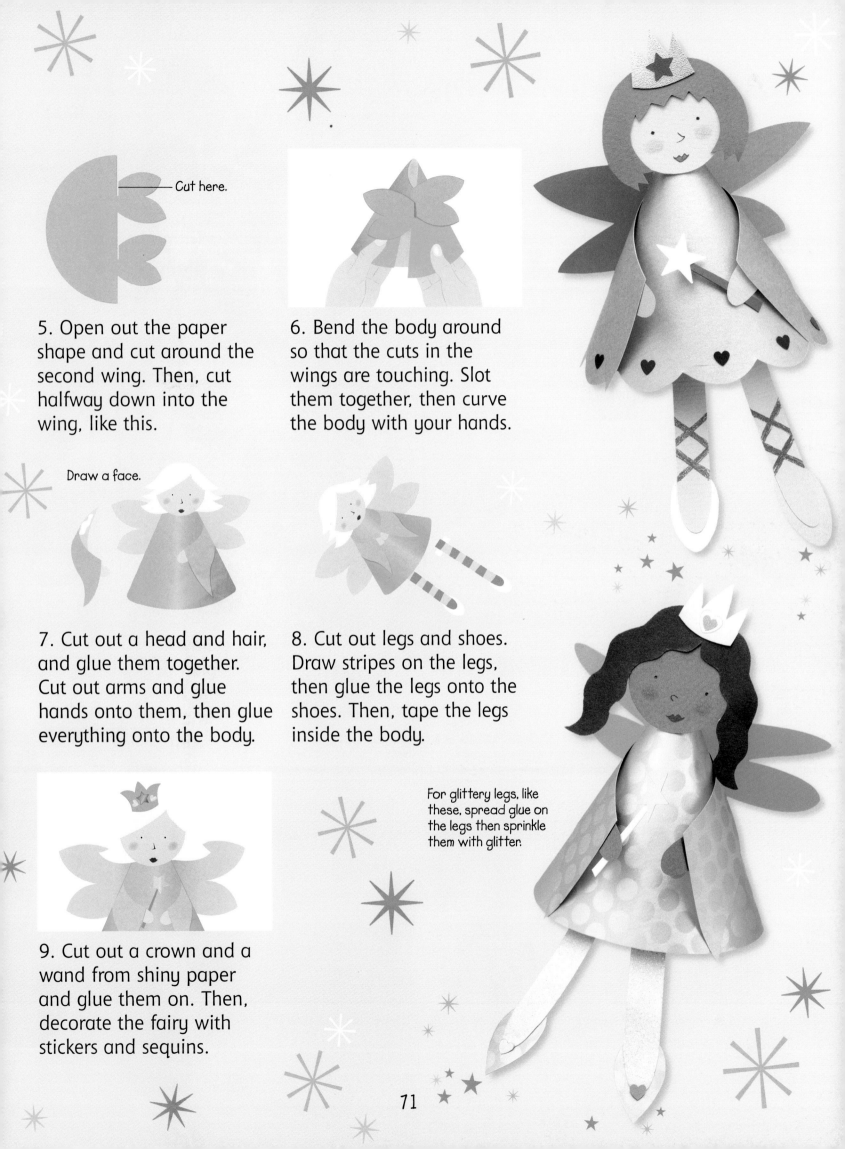

— Cut here.

5. Open out the paper shape and cut around the second wing. Then, cut halfway down into the wing, like this.

6. Bend the body around so that the cuts in the wings are touching. Slot them together, then curve the body with your hands.

Draw a face.

7. Cut out a head and hair, and glue them together. Cut out arms and glue hands onto them, then glue everything onto the body.

8. Cut out legs and shoes. Draw stripes on the legs, then glue the legs onto the shoes. Then, tape the legs inside the body.

For glittery legs, like these, spread glue on the legs then sprinkle them with glitter.

9. Cut out a crown and a wand from shiny paper and glue them on. Then, decorate the fairy with stickers and sequins.

Sparkly decorations

1. Cut a piece of thread that is about the length of a pencil. Then, cut four strips of kitchen foil about the same length.

2. Fold the thread in half and lay the ends on one of the strips of foil. Scrunch the foil into a ball around the ends and squeeze hard.

Make lots of decorations on a long piece of thread and make a loop at the top.

Roll the ball on a flat surface.

3. Squeeze the other strips of foil around the first one, to make a ball. Then, roll the ball under your hand, to make it round.

4. Brush half of the ball with household glue (PVA) and sprinkle glitter over it. Leave it to dry, then cover the other half with glitter.

72

Christmas cards
and
wrapping paper

Shiny bauble card

1. For a long card, fold a rectangle of thick paper in half, with its long sides together, and crease the fold well.

Use stickers from the sticker pages to decorate some of the baubles.

The strings on these cards were drawn with gold and silver pens.

Use shiny paper
if you have it.

2. Draw around several small jar lids on the back of pieces of wrapping paper. Cut out the circles you have drawn.

3. For a striped bauble, cut strips of shiny paper. Glue them across one of the circles, letting the strips overlap the edges.

4. When the glue is dry, turn the bauble over. Then, cut off the ends of the strips which overlap the edge of the circle.

5. To make a bauble with stars, press stickers onto one of your shiny circles. Make some of them overlap the edges.

6. Trim off all the extra pieces of the stickers which are overlapping the edges of the circle, as you did before.

7. Decorate the other shiny circles with different patterns of stripes, stars and circles. Use stickers or cut shapes from paper.

8. Glue the circles onto the card at different levels. Use a felt-tip pen to draw a string from the top of the card to each bauble.

Polar bear pop-up card

The pieces of paper should be the same size.

1. Fold a piece of white or cream paper in half. Do the same with a piece of blue paper.

2. On the white or cream paper, draw half of a bear's head against the fold, like this.

Keep the paper folded as you cut.

Nose cut

3. Cut around the head. Make a cut for a nose. Cut out shapes along the edge for fur, too.

The polar bear pops up in the middle of the card. You'll need to decorate the front too.

Follow the steps on page 88 for a glitter star.

4. Lift the nose and fold it flat onto the front, like this. Crease the fold. Fold it behind, too.

5. Open out the head. Push a finger through the nose from the back, so that it stands up.

Press on a sticker from the sticker pages.

Glue on a paper shape (see page 36). Dab on thick white paint for snow. Sprinkle it with sugar.

6. Use felt-tip pens to draw a mouth and eyes. Carefully fill in the nose.

7. Put glue on the back of the head, but not on the nose. Press the head onto the blue paper.

8. Cut a rectangle of wrapping paper for a present. Glue it on below the head.

9. Cut two paws from white paper. Glue them on. Add claws with a black felt-tip pen.

Sparkling card

1. Cut two squares of clear book covering film. Make them the same size. Then, peel the backing paper off one of them.

2. Lay the film on a table, sticky-side up. Press lots of sequins and little pieces of thread onto the film. Then, sprinkle on some glitter.

3. Peel the backing paper off the other piece of film and lay it, sticky-side down, on the decorated piece of film.

These cards really sparkle if you sprinkle lots of glitter over the film.

4. Fold a piece of thick paper in half. Open it out again and draw around the film, on the left-hand side, like this.

5. Push a sharp pencil into the middle of the shape to make a hole. Then, push the blade of some scissors into the hole.

78

6. Cut a 'window' in the paper, smaller than the shape you drew. Don't worry if the sides don't make a perfect square.

Here are some ideas of different shapes of 'windows' cut into some cards.

7. Glue around the 'window', then press on the decorated film. Then, cut a square of paper and glue it over the film.

You could use this technique to make gift tags too.

Santa card

1. Fold a square of thick paper in half to make a card. Cut a curved hat from red paper and glue it near the top.

2. Cut a beard with a wavy outline from white paper. Glue it on the card below the hat, leaving a gap between the two.

3. Cut a wavy strip from white paper and glue it on the hat. Press on a white sticker too, or cut one from paper.

4. Cut out a nose from red paper and glue it on. Press on two stickers for eyes. Then, add a smile with a red felt-tip pen.

Try cutting out different shapes of Santa hats.

Tree card

1. Cut a big rectangle of thick paper or thin cardboard. Fold it in half, long sides together.

Save this half for later.

2. Get some help to cut a large potato in half from end to end. Cut one half into a tall triangle.

Spread the paint with the back of a spoon.

3. Lay some kitchen paper towels onto some old newspapers. Pour green paint on top.

Dip the potato into the paint each time you print a shape.

4. Dip the potato into the paint and press it onto your card. Print more trees along the card.

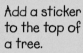

Add a sticker to the top of a tree.

Print a row of trees on bright paper.

5. Cut a square of potato. Dip it in red paint and print it below each tree.

Painted snow fairy card

1. For the card, fold a piece of blue paper in half. Then, lay a mug on a piece of white paper. Draw around it, then cut out the circle.

2. Mix some paint for the fairy's face and body. Paint a face on the circle. Then, paint a body below it, like this.

3. Paint four shapes for the fairy's wings. Then, paint the hair and a small yellow circle for the end of the wand.

You could paint little white dots around the circle, instead of printing snowflakes.

Try painting fairies with their wands and arms in different positions.

4. When the paint is dry, outline the fairy's body, chin and wings with a black felt-tip pen. Decorate her dress, too.

5. Draw a face, then add arms, legs and lines on the fairy's hair. Then, draw a wand with a star on the end, like this.

6. Glue the circle onto the folded card. Then, paint a thin white line down from the top of the card and add a bow.

You could print a mixture of snowflakes and dots on the card.

7. To print the snowflakes, cut a small piece of thick cardboard. Dip the end of it into some white paint, then press it onto the card.

8. Print a second line across the first one and add a third line. Print lots more snowflakes around the circle.

Zigzag card

1. Cut a long, thin rectangle of thick paper or very thin cardboard. Fold it in half lengthways and crease the fold well.

To make the card stand up, pull the front layer forward to make a zigzag.

Middle fold

2. Fold the top layer over until it meets the middle fold. Turn the card over and fold it in the same way, to make a zigzag.

3. Open the card and draw a wavy line from one side of the card to the other, like this. Use a pencil and press lightly.

4. Cut along the line you have drawn but stop at the last fold. Then, cut down the fold from the top, as far as the pencil line.

The shapes are shown in yellow here so you can see them.

5. Fold the card into a zigzag again. Then, use a white wax crayon to draw some stars and a moon. Press hard as you draw.

6. Open the card, then paint over the stars and moon with blue paint as far as the pencil line. The shapes will resist the paint.

7. While the sky is drying, draw lots of dots on some thick paper with the white wax crayon. Then, paint green paint over the top.

If you want to draw lines on the trees, like those on two of these cards, cut out the triangles before you draw them at step 7.

Overlap the little trees.

8. When the paint is dry, cut out about eight little triangles for the trees. Make them slightly different sizes.

9. Glue three of the trees onto the back layer of the card. Then, glue another one on the layer in front, like this.

10. Lay the rest of the trees on the top two layers so that they don't overlap any of the other trees. Then, glue them on.

Reindeer wrapping paper

1. Use a crayon to draw the body. Add a neck.

2. Draw the head and add two ears.

3. Add four long legs and a tail.

4. Crayon hooves, a nose and two eyes.

5. Draw jagged antlers on its head.

6. Add spikes to the antlers. Fill in with pens.

Make a long thin card.

Make a gift tag to match the paper.

To draw a fir tree

1. Draw the trunk of a tree with a crayon.

2. Add branches with a wax crayon.

Draw lots of reindeer and trees on small pieces of paper. Then, glue them onto a large piece of bright wrapping paper.

3. Draw dark green branches over the top.

Tie some ribbon around your present.

Gift tags

Stars

1. Press the sharp edge of a star-shaped cookie cutter into half a potato. Press it in well.

2. Spread thick paint on an old plate. Press the star into the paint then press it onto thin cardboard.

You could write a name in the middle of the star.

3. Before the paint dries, sprinkle it with lots of glitter. Then, shake off any extra glitter.

4. When it's dry, cut around the star, a little way away from the glitter. Tape a ribbon on the back.

Snowmen

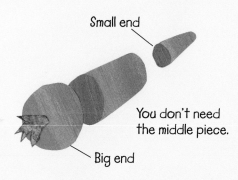

Small end

You don't need the middle piece.

Big end

1. Cut the ends off a big, thick carrot, so that you have a big end and a small one.

2. Dip the big end of the carrot into thick paint. Then, press it onto thin cardboard, for a body.

Use pens to draw the face, hat and buttons.

3. Print a head with the small end. When it's dry, draw on eyes, a nose, mouth, a hat and buttons.

Round tags

Put the paint on an old plate.

1. Dip the edge of a piece of thick cardboard into gold paint. Print a criss-cross pattern on thin cardboard.

2. When the paint is dry, put a small lid onto the piece of cardboard and draw around it. Cut out the circle.

3. Use felt-tip pens to decorate the circle. Draw stripes and zigzags. Tape ribbon on the back.

Try drawing different faces on the snowman tags.

89

Printed star wrapping paper

Make the slice as thick as your thumb.

1. You will need a large cookie cutter and a potato, which is bigger than the cutter.

2. Carefully cut a slice from the middle of the potato. Press the cookie cutter into the slice.

3. Push out the shape you have cut. You may need some help with the last two steps.

Try printing with gold or silver poster paint.

4. Dab both sides of the potato shape on some kitchen paper towels to dry it.

5. Press a fork into the shape. This will stop you from getting too messy when you print.

6. Pour two or three small patches of paint onto an old newspaper. Do them close together.

You could wrap your presents in your printed paper and tie a shiny ribbon around them.

7. Dip the potato shape into the middle of the paint, then press it onto a piece of paper.

8. Dip the shape into the paint again, then print it. Fill the paper with lots of printed shapes.

The papers below were printed with a potato cut with a Christmas tree cookie cutter.

Snowman card

Press star stickers in the sky around the snowman.

You could add stick arms with a felt-tip pen.

Cut a hat from black paper and glue it on.

92

1. Cut a rectangle from blue paper. Then, cut a piece of thick white paper exactly the same size. Fold both of them in half.

2. Open the blue paper. Draw a wavy line across one side of the card for snow. Draw the outline of a snowman on the line.

3. Use scissors to cut along the line for the snow, then around the snowman and along the line for snow again.

4. Spread glue over the bottom half of the blue card. Then, press one side of the white card onto it, matching the edges.

5. Spread glue over the top of the blue card, around the snowman. Then, close the card, pressing it down onto the white card.

This card had two snowman shapes drawn on the wavy line (see step 2).

6. Draw eyes and a line of dots for the mouth. Add a nose and a hat and press on stickers for buttons.

Spots and stars card

1. Cut two small potatoes in half. Then, use an old spoon to spread a patch of white paint onto a pile of kitchen paper towels.

2. Dip the cut side of one of the potatoes into the paint. Press it onto a large piece of red paper, then lift it off.

3. Dip the potato into the paint again and do another print. Do this lots of times until the paper is covered in white spots.

Use a different potato for each paint.

4. Spread some silver and blue paint onto the paper towels and print lots more spots. Make some of them overlap the white ones.

5. For the circles, dip the edge of a bottle top into one of the paints and print it, overlapping some of the spots.

Instead of making cards, you could use the whole sheet of paper as wrapping paper.

6. For the stars, dip the edge of a piece of cardboard into some paint and print a line. Print two more lines in an 'X' on top.

7. Leave the paint to dry, then cut the paper into several rectangles. Fold each rectangle in half to make a card.

You could cut out a circle as a gift tag and attach it to a present with a ribbon.

Wrapping ideas

Spotted paper and tag

1. Wrap your present. Then, rip lots of circles from a different piece of wrapping paper.

2. Glue the circles all over the wrapped present. Make the circles bend over the edges of the present.

3. Rip lots of smaller circles from a different colour of paper. Then, glue them onto the bigger circles.

Springy gift tags

1. Cut a star from thin cardboard. Decorate it with felt-tip pens, stickers or glitter.

2. Wind a pipe cleaner tightly around a pencil or felt-tip pen. Then, slide it off gently.

3. Push the last two coils of the pipe cleaner together at one end. Glue it to the back of the star.

4. Do the same to the coils at the other end. Put some glue on it and press it on your present.

Make a springy gift tag which matches your wrapping paper.

Tissue paper present

Press shiny star stickers onto each circle.

1. Cut a large square from a double layer of tissue paper. Lay your present in the middle.

Use tissue paper to wrap oddly shaped presents, such as a mug.

2. Gather the paper up around the present, then tie it tightly with a piece of gift ribbon.

For a different springy tag, cut out a Christmas tree and decorate it with felt-tip pens or stickers.

Star card

Shake off the extra glitter when the glue is dry.

1. Draw three stars on a piece of bright paper and cut them out.

2. Put a blob of glue on each star and sprinkle it with glitter.

3. Cut three strips of thin paper. Glue a strip to the back of each star.

Glue under here.

4. Fold a piece of thick paper in half. Glue the stars onto it, like this.

Cut out a tree shape. Make lots of stars and glue them on.

5. When the glue is dry, stand the card up. The stars fall forward.

Tape a star onto a present. Write a name on it.

Christmas cooking

Little Christmas trees

To make 10 trees and 16 presents, you will need:
275g (9½oz) self-raising flour
225g (8oz) soft margarine
4 tablespoons milk
1 level teaspoon of baking powder
225g (8oz) caster sugar
2-3 drops vanilla essence
4 medium eggs

For the butter icing:
75g (3oz) butter, softened
175g (6oz) icing sugar
2 teaspoons lemon juice
food dyes

You could arrange the presents around the trees.

Heat the oven to 180°C, 350°F, gas mark 4, before you start.

Use a paper towel to wipe oil on the tin.

Use a roasting tin.

Use a wooden spoon.

1. Draw around a tin on greaseproof paper. Cut it out. Wipe oil inside the tin. Put the paper into the tin and oil the paper.

2. Sift the flour into a large mixing bowl. Add the margarine, milk, baking powder, sugar and vanilla essence.

3. Break the eggs into a small bowl. Beat them with a fork. Add them to the flour mixture. Beat everything together well.

Make trunks for the trees from chocolate bars or biscuits.

100

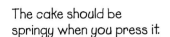

The cake should be springy when you press it.

4. Spoon the mixture into the tin. Smooth the top. Bake it in the oven for 40-45 minutes, until the middle is springy.

5. Leave the cake in the tin to cool, then lift it out. Put the butter into a bowl. Beat it with a wooden spoon until it is creamy.

6. Sift in the icing sugar and stir it in, a little at a time. Stir in the lemon juice. Put three-quarters of the icing in a bowl.

To make the colour stronger, add more dye, a drop at a time.

These will be the presents.

7. Mix in a little green food dye. Divide the rest of the icing into three bowls. Mix a drop of food dye into each one.

8. Cut a strip 7cm (3in) wide from one end of the cake. Cut it into 16 small squares. Cut the cake in half along its length.

9. Cut out ten triangles. Ice them with green icing. Ice the presents with the other icing. Press sweets onto the cakes.

Decorate the trees with sweets.

...t mice

...ght large mice, five medium
...e baby mice, you will need:
...oz) icing sugar, sifted
...oz) tin of condensed milk
...(7oz) desiccated coconut
red food dye
sweets for ears
...ilver cake-decorating balls
liquorice 'bootlaces'

1. Mix the icing sugar and
the condensed milk
together in a bowl. Mix
in the coconut. Put the
mixture into two bowls.

2. Add a few drops of red
dye to each bowl and mix
it in. Then add a few
more drops of dye to
one of the bowls.

For baby mice,
use a teaspoon
for the body.

3. Dip a clean tablespoon into some warm water and let it drip a little. Then, lift out a big spoonful of the mixture.

4. Pat the spoonful smooth on top. Turn the spoon over and put the shape onto a piece of plastic foodwrap.

5. Pinch a nose at the thinner end of the spoon shape. Then, add sweets for ears and silver balls for eyes.

6. Push a piece of liquorice under the shape, as a tail. Leave the mouse to harden on a plate. Make lots more mice from the mixture.

Use a dessertspoon for a medium mouse.

Cheesy Christmas stars

To make about 25 stars, you will need:
150g (6oz) self-raising flour
half a teaspoon of salt
75g (3oz) butter or margarine
75g (3oz) cheese, finely grated
1 egg and 1 tablespoon of milk, beaten together
a star-shaped cutter
a greased baking sheet

Heat the oven to 200°C, 400°F, gas mark 6,
before you start.

1. Sift the flour and salt through a sieve. Add the butter or margarine and rub it with your fingers to make fine crumbs.

2. Leave a tablespoon of the grated cheese on a saucer. Add the rest of the cheese to the bowl and stir it in.

3. Put a tablespoon of the beaten egg and milk mixture into a cup. Mix the rest into the flour to make a dough.

Use a rolling pin.

Use a pastry brush.

4. Sprinkle flour onto a clean work surface. Roll out the dough, until it is slightly thinner than your little finger.

5. Use the cutter to cut out lots of star shapes. Cut them close together. Make the scraps into a ball, and roll them out.

6. Cut out more stars. Brush the stars with the rest of the egg mixture, then sprinkle them with the rest of the cheese.

7. Put the stars onto the greased baking sheet. Bake them in the oven for eight to ten minutes, until they are golden.

These stars are delicious to eat when they are warm.

Creamy chocolate fudge

To make about 36 squares of fudge, you will need:
75g (3oz) full-fat cream cheese
350g (12oz) icing sugar
1 level tablespoon of cocoa powder
1 teaspoon of oil, for wiping
75g (3oz) plain chocolate drops
40g (1½oz) butter
a shallow 15cm (6in) square cake tin
greaseproof paper

You could wrap the fudge and give it as a Christmas present.

Use a pencil to draw around the tin.

1. Put the cream cheese into a bowl. Sift the icing sugar and cocoa through a sieve into the bowl too. Mix them together well.

2. Put the cake tin onto a sheet of greaseproof paper and draw around it. Cut out the shape, just inside the line.

3. Use a paper towel to wipe oil onto the sides and base of the tin. Press in the paper square and wipe it too.

4. Melt the chocolate and butter as in steps 1-3 on page 118. Then, stir in a tablespoon of the cream cheese mixture.

5. Pour the chocolate into the cheese mixture in the bowl. Beat them together with a spoon until they are creamy.

6. Spoon the mixture into the tin, and push it into the corners. Make the top of the fudge as flat as you can.

7. Smooth the top of the fudge with the back of a spoon. Put the tin in the fridge for two hours, or until the fudge is firm.

8. Use a blunt knife to loosen the edges of the fudge, then turn it out onto a large plate. Remove the paper.

9. Cut the fudge into lots of squares. Then, put the plate in the fridge for two hours, until the fudge is hard.

Crinkly Christmas pies

To make 12 pies, you will need:
4 eating apples
3 tablespoons orange juice or cold water
50g (2oz) dried cranberries or sultanas
2 teaspoons caster sugar
half a teaspoon of ground cinnamon
100g (4oz) filo pastry (about 6 sheets)
50g (2oz) butter
2 teaspoons icing sugar
a baking tray with shallow pans or 12-hole muffin tin

Heat the oven to 190°C, 375°F, gas mark 5, before you start.

You may need to ask someone to help you.

1. Peel the apples. Cut them into quarters and cut out the cores. Cut them into small pieces and put them in the pan.

Put the lid back on after you've stirred the apples.

2. Add the juice or water and put the pan on a very low heat. Cover it with a lid. Cook for 20 minutes, stirring often.

Stir the mixture often.

3. Stir in the fruit, caster sugar and cinnamon. Cook the mixture for about five minutes, then take it off the heat.

Keep the six sheets together.

4. Take the pan off the heat. Unwrap the pastry and cut all the sheets into six squares. Cover them with foodwrap.

Use a pastry brush.

5. Put the butter in a small pan and melt it over a low heat. Brush a little butter over one of the pastry squares.

6. Put the square into a hole in the tray, buttered side up. Press it gently into the hole. Brush butter onto another square.

Overlap the pastry sheets so that they look like a star.

7. Put this square over the first one. Overlap the corners slightly. Butter and add a third square. Repeat in all the holes.

Heat the apples until they bubble a little.

Eat the pies warm or cold.

8. Put the tray on the middle shelf of the oven and cook for 10 minutes. Take it out and leave it to cool for five minutes.

9. Take the pastry cases out of the tray and put them onto a large plate. Heat the apples again for about two minutes.

10. Spoon the apple mixture into the pastry cases, so that they are almost full. Sift icing sugar onto them.

Painted biscuits

To make about 15 biscuits, you will need:
50g (2oz) icing sugar
75g (3oz) soft margarine
the yolk from a large egg
vanilla essence
150g (5oz) plain flour
plastic foodwrap
big cutters
a greased baking sheet

To decorate the biscuits:
an egg yolk
food dyes

Heat the oven to 180°C, 350°F,
gas mark 4, before you start.

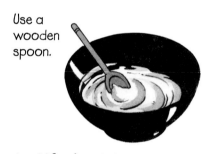

Use a
wooden
spoon.

1. Sift the icing sugar
through a sieve into a large
bowl. Add the margarine
and mix well until they are
smooth.

2. Add the large egg yolk
and stir it in well. Then,
add a few drops of vanilla
essence. Stir the vanilla
into the mixture.

3. Hold a sieve over the
bowl and pour the flour
into it. Sift the flour
through the sieve, to
remove any lumps.

4. Mix in the flour until
you get a smooth dough.
Wrap the dough in plastic
foodwrap and put it in the
freezer.

Decorate your biscuits with lots of different patterns.

It takes time to decorate the biscuits, so you could freeze some of the dough to use another day.

5. Put the egg yolk into a bowl and beat it with a fork. Put it onto saucers. Mix a few drops of food dye into each one.

6. Take the dough out of the freezer. Roll out half of it onto a floury work surface, until it is as thin as your little finger.

7. Press out shapes with cutters. Use a fish slice to lift them onto a baking sheet. Roll out the rest of the dough.

8. Cut out more shapes. Use a clean paintbrush to paint shapes on the biscuits with the egg and dye mixture.

9. Bake the biscuits for 10-12 minutes. Remove them from the oven. Let them cool a little, then lift them onto a wire rack.

y jam tart

To make one jam tart, you will need:

(12oz) packet shortcrust pastry
about 2 tablespoons plain flour
tablespoons seedless raspberry or
strawberry jam
1 tablespoon of milk
20cm (8in) fluted flan tin
a small star-shaped cutter

en to 200°C, 400°F, gas mark 6, before you start.

You can use any shape
of cutter you like.
Stars and holly leaves
look very Christmassy.

1. Take the pastry out of the fridge and leave it for 10 minutes. Sprinkle a clean work surface with some flour.

2. Cut off quarter of the pastry and wrap it in some plastic foodwrap. Sprinkle some flour onto a rolling pin.

Sift a slice of tart with a little icing sugar and serve it with cream.

The rolling pin cuts off the extra pastry.

3. Roll out the bigger piece of pastry. Turn it a little, then roll it again. Make a circle about 30cm (12in) across.

4. Put the rolling pin at one side of the pastry. Roll the pastry around it and lift it up. Place it over the tin and unroll it.

5. Dip a finger into some flour and press the pastry into the edges of the tin. Then, roll the rolling pin across the top.

6. Spoon the jam into the pastry case. Spread it out with the back of a spoon. Roll out the other quarter of the pastry.

7. Using the cutter, cut out about 12 pastry shapes. Brush them with a little milk and place them on top of the jam.

The pastry should be golden brown.

8. Put the jam tart in the oven. Bake it for about 20 minutes. Take the tart from the oven and let the jam cool before serving.

Peppermint creams

To make about 25 peppermint creams, you will need:
250g (9oz) icing sugar
half the white of a small egg, mixed from dried
egg white (mix as directed on the packet)
1 teaspoon peppermint flavouring
2 teaspoons lemon juice
green food dye
a rolling pin
small cutters
a baking sheet covered in
plastic foodwrap

Put peppermint
creams in boxes,
to give as presents.

1. Sift the icing sugar through a sieve into a large bowl. Make a hole in the middle of the sugar with a spoon.

2. Mix the egg white, peppermint flavouring and lemon juice in a small bowl. Pour the mixture into the sugar.

3. Use a blunt knife to stir the mixture. Then, squeeze it between your fingers until it is smooth, like a dough.

4. Cut the mixture into two pieces. Put each piece into a bowl. Add a few drops of green food dye to one bowl.

5. Use your fingers to mix in the dye. If the mixture is sticky, add a little more icing sugar and mix it in.

6. Sprinkle a little icing sugar onto a clean work surface. Sprinkle some onto a rolling pin too, to stop the mixture sticking.

Cut the shapes close together.

7. Roll out the green mixture until it is about as thick as your little finger. Use cutters to cut out lots of shapes.

8. Use a blunt knife to lift the shapes onto the baking sheet. Roll out the white mixture and cut out more shapes.

9. Lift all the shapes onto the baking sheet. Leave them for at least an hour until they become hard.

Shortbread

To make eight pieces, you will need:
butter for greasing
150g (5oz) plain flour
25g (1oz) rice flour or ground rice
100g (4oz) butter, refrigerated, cut into chunks
50g (2oz) caster sugar
a 20cm (8in) shallow round tin

Heat the oven to 150°C, 300°F, gas mark 2, before you start.

1. Grease the bottom and sides of the round tin with some butter on a piece of paper towel. Make sure it is all greased.

2. Sift the flour and rice flour or ground rice through a sieve into a large bowl. Add the butter to the bowl.

3. Mix in the butter so that it is coated in flour. Rub it into the flour with your fingers until it is like fine breadcrumbs.

4. Stir in the sugar with a wooden spoon. Hold the bowl with one hand and squeeze the mixture into a ball with the other.

5. Press the mixture into the tin with your fingers. Use the back of a spoon to smooth the top and make it level.

6. Use a fork to press patterns around the edge and holes in the middle. Cut the shortbread into eight pieces.

7. Bake the shortbread for 30 minutes, until it is golden. After 10 minutes, take it out of the tin. Put it on a wire rack to cool.

Chocolate truffles

To make about 10 truffles, you will need:
100g (4oz) plain or white chocolate drops
25g (1oz) butter
25g (1oz) icing sugar
50g (2oz) plain cake, crumbled into fine crumbs
2 tablespoons desiccated coconut
2 tablespoons chocolate sugar strands
small paper cases for sweets

1. Pour water into a pan, until it is about 3cm (1in) deep. Heat it until it bubbles, then remove the pan from the heat.

2. Put the chocolate drops and the butter into a heatproof bowl. Put on oven gloves and gently put the bowl in the pan.

Ask someone to help you to lift the bowl.

3. Stir the chocolate and butter together until they have melted. Using oven gloves, carefully lift the bowl out of the water.

4. Sift the icing sugar through a sieve into the chocolate. Add the cake crumbs and stir until everything is well mixed.

The white truffles
are covered with
desiccated coconut.

5. Leave the mixture to cool. Put the desiccated coconut onto one plate, and the chocolate strands onto another.

6. When the mixture is firm and thick, scoop up some with a teaspoon. Put the spoonful into the coconut or strands.

Roll the spoonful to make a ball.

7. Roll the spoonful of chocolate around until it is covered, then put it in a paper case. Make lots more truffles.

8. Put the truffles onto a large plate. Put the plate in the fridge for 30 minutes, or until the truffles are firm.

Shining star biscuits

To make about 20 biscuits, you will need:
50g (2oz) light soft brown sugar
50g (2oz) butter, softened
a small egg
115g (4½oz) plain flour
15g (½oz) cornflour
1 teaspoon ground mixed spice
solid boiled sweets
a large star-shaped cutter
a fat drinking straw
a small round cutter, slightly bigger than the sweets
a large baking tray lined with baking parchment

Heat the oven to 180°C, 350°F, gas mark 4, before you start.

Thread thin ribbon through the holes.

1. Using a wooden spoon, mix the sugar and butter together really well, getting rid of any lumps in the mixture.

2. Break the egg into a separate bowl. Beat the egg with a fork until the yolk and the white are mixed together.

3. Mix half of the beaten egg into the mixture in the bowl, a little at a time. You don't need the other half of the egg mixture.

4. Sift the flour, cornflour and mixed spice through a sieve. Mix everything together really well with a wooden spoon.

5. Squeeze the mixture with your hands until a firm dough is formed. Make the dough into a large ball.

6. Sprinkle a clean work surface with a little flour. Then, roll out the ball of dough until it is 5mm (¼in) thick.

If you hang biscuits on a Christmas tree, don't eat them afterwards.

7. Line the baking tray with baking parchment. Use a large cutter to cut out stars. Use a fish slice to put them onto the tray.

8. Make a hole in each star shape by pressing the straw through the dough, near to the top of one of the points.

9. Use a small round cutter to cut a hole in the middle of each star. The hole should be slightly bigger than the sweet.

10. Squeeze the leftover pieces of dough into a ball. Roll them out. Cut out more stars. Put them on the baking tray.

11. Drop a sweet into the hole in the middle of each star shape. Put the baking tray on the middle shelf of the oven.

12. Bake the shapes for twelve minutes, then take them out. Leave them on the baking tray until they are completely cold.

Snowmen and presents

To make lots of snowmen and presents, you will need:
250g (9oz) 'white' marzipan*
green, red and yellow food dyes
toothpicks

Colouring marzipan

Add a little icing sugar if the marzipan gets too sticky.

1. Unwrap the marzipan. Then, put it on a plate and cut it into quarters. Put each quarter into a small bowl.

2. Add one drop of green food dye, then mix it in with your fingers. Carry on until the marzipan is evenly coloured.

3. Leave one quarter of the marzipan 'white'. Add red food dye to one quarter, and yellow to the other. Mix in the dye.

A snowman

Put the marzipan balls on a plate.

Press the ball with your thumb.

Cross the ends of the scarf.

1. Roll a piece of 'white' marzipan into a ball. Then, make a smaller ball. Press the smaller ball onto the larger one.

2. Roll a small ball of red marzipan. Press it to make a circle. Put it on the snowman's head. Put a tiny red ball on top.

3. Roll a thin sausage from red marzipan. Wrap it around the snowman for a scarf. Press in a face with a toothpick.

* Marzipan contains ground nuts. Don't make these if you are allergic to nuts.

Ice a cake with butter icing (see pages 100-101) and decorate it with snowmen and presents.

A present

1. Roll a ball of red marzipan and put it on a work surface. Gently press the flat side of a knife down on the ball.

2. Turn the ball on its side and press it with the knife again. Keep on doing this until the ball becomes a cube.

3. Roll thin sausages of green marzipan. Press them onto the cube, in a cross. Add two loops in the middle for a bow.

Iced gingerbread hearts

To make about 20 biscuits, you will need:
350g (12oz) plain flour
2 teaspoons ground ginger
1 teaspoon of bicarbonate of soda
100g (4oz) butter or margarine, cut into chunks
175g (6oz) soft light brown sugar
1 medium egg
4 tablespoons golden syrup
white writing icing
silver cake-decorating balls
a large heart-shaped cutter
2 greased baking trays

Heat the oven to 190°C, 375°F, gas mark 5, before you start.

You could wrap some biscuits in tissue paper or cellophane twists, to give as a present.

1. Sift the flour, ground ginger and bicarbonate of soda into a large bowl. Add the butter or margarine chunks.

2. Rub the butter or margarine into the flour with your fingers until it is like fine breadcrumbs. Stir in the sugar.

3. Break the egg into a small bowl, then add the syrup. Beat well with a fork, then stir the egg mixture into the flour.

4. Mix with a metal spoon until you make a dough. Sprinkle flour onto a work surface, then put the dough on it.

5. Stretch the dough by pushing it away from you. Fold it in half and repeat. Carry on doing this until it is smooth.

6. Sprinkle more flour onto the work surface. Cut the dough in half. Then, roll out one half until it is 5mm (¼in) thick.

7. Use a cookie cutter to cut out lots of hearts. Then, lift all the hearts onto the greased baking trays with a fish slice.

8. Roll out the rest of the dough and cut out more hearts. Put them on the baking trays, then put the baking trays in the oven.

9. Bake the biscuits for 12-15 minutes. They will turn golden brown. Carefully lift the baking trays from the oven.

10. Leave the biscuits on the trays for about 5 minutes. Then, lift them onto a wire rack. Leave them to cool.

11. When the biscuits are cold, draw lines across them with the icing. Cross some of the lines over each other.

12. Leave the icing to harden a little. Then, push in a silver cake-decorating ball where the lines of icing cross.

Christmas tree cakes

To make 15 cakes, you will need:
100g (4oz) self-raising flour
2 medium eggs
100g (4oz) soft margarine
100g (4oz) caster sugar
paper cake cases
2 baking trays with shallow pans
small sweets for decorating

For the butter icing:
75g (3oz) butter or margarine, softened
175g (6oz) icing sugar, sifted
2 teaspoons lemon juice or a few
drops of vanilla essence

Heat the oven to 190°C, 375°F, gas mark 5,
before you start.

1. Break the eggs into a cup. Then, sift the flour through a sieve into a big bowl. Add the eggs, margarine and sugar.

2. Stir everything together really well with a wooden spoon. Carry on stirring until you get a smooth creamy mixture.

3. Put the paper cases into the pans in the baking trays. Use a spoon to half-fill each case with the mixture.

Stir it very quickly.

4. Bake the cakes for about 20 minutes and carefully take them out of the oven. Leave them on a rack to cool.

5. To make the icing, put the butter or margarine into a bowl and stir it with a fork. Carry on until it is really creamy.

6. Add some of the icing sugar to the butter and stir it in. Mix in the rest of the icing sugar, a little at a time.

7. Stir the lemon juice or vanilla essence into the mixture. Add a little more lemon juice or vanilla if the icing is very thick.

Arrange the cakes into a tree shape, like this.

8. Spread some butter icing on the top of each cake. Use the sweets to make different patterns on each cake.

Use a flaky chocolate bar as a tree trunk.

Index